LOST
TREASURES

by Cynthia O'Brien

Crabtree Publishing Company
www.crabtreebooks.com

Crabtree Publishing Company
www.crabtreebooks.com

Author: Cynthia O'Brien
Project Editor: Tim Cooke
Designer: Lynne Lennon
Picture Researcher: Andrew Webb
Picture Manager: Sophie Mortimer
Art Director: Keith Davis
Editorial Director: Lindsey Lowe
Children's Publisher: Anne O'Daly
Editor: Kelly Spence
Proofreader: Kathy Middleton
Cover Design: Margaret Amy Salter
**Production Coordinator and
    Prepress Technician:** Ken Wright
Print Coordinator: Margaret Amy Salter

Photographs
Cover: Shutterstock
Interior: Alamy: Everett Collection Historical: 15,
North Wind Pictures 9; Ancient Art & Architecture Collection: 11;
Associated Press: 17; Dreamstime: Bambi L. Dingman 7; Howard Pyle:
8, 20; Jennyfan: 29; Library of Congress: 24, 27; Lost Dutchman Rare
Coins: 26; Mike Peel: 19; National Maritime Museum: 16; OakIsland.
com: 21; Shutterstock: Andrey Armyagov 4, Garanga 22, Mark Skalny
6, James Steidl 12, Marin Veraja 23; Thinkstock: iStockphoto Photos.
com 14, Photodisc 25; Robert Hunt Library: 28.

Every attempt to contact copyright holders has been made by the
publisher.

Library and Archives Canada Cataloguing in Publication

O'Brien, Cynthia (Cynthia J.), author
    Lost treasures / Cynthia O'Brien.

(Mystery files)
Includes index.
Issued in print and electronic formats.
ISBN 978-0-7787-8071-7 (bound).--ISBN 978-0-7787-8075-5 (pbk.).--
ISBN 978-1-4271-9968-3 (pdf).--ISBN 978-1-4271-9964-5 (html)

    1. Treasure troves--Juvenile literature. I. Title.

G525.O27 2015   j622'.19   C2014-908105-7
                                         C2014-908106-5

Library of Congress Cataloging-in-Publication Data

CIP available at the Library of Congress

Crabtree Publishing Company
www.crabtreebooks.com   1-800-387-7650

Published in Canada
Crabtree Publishing
616 Welland Ave.
St. Catharines, ON
L2M 5V6

Published in the United States
Crabtree Publishing
PMB 59051
350 Fifth Avenue, 59th Floor
New York, New York 10118

Published by **CRABTREE PUBLISHING COMPANY in 2015**
Copyright © 2015 Brown Bear Books Ltd

In Canada: We acknowledge the financial support of the Government of
Canada through the Canada Book Fund for our publishing activities.

Printed in Canada/022015/MA20150101

Contents

Introduction

Since ancient times, people have been fascinated by stories of lost treasure. These stories include tales of ancient gold and silver that was buried for safekeeping or sealed in tombs with its dead owners. Legends tell of buried treasure hidden by **pirates** on desert islands, and priceless treasures having been lost during shipwrecks or the chaos of war.

Most tales of vanished treasures are nothing but rumors. A few, however, proved to be true. Some treasure hunters have made fortunes. Others have wasted their money and their time.

Everyone dreams of finding a map that will lead them to treasure.

In ancient times, people often buried their money to keep it safe.

Treasure hunters have tried to interpret maps, notes, and **cryptic** messages to find secret places that may hide a mysterious fortune. Many people have risked their lives in search of riches—and many of these lost treasures are still waiting to be discovered!

Missing Millions

In the following pages, find out about pirate **loot** and gold protected by an ancient curse. Learn the story behind a Mexican bandit and his missing silver. Then discover the exciting tale of a farmer's son who found a buried stash of Roman coins with a metal detector!

Mystery words...

cryptic: unclear or secret meaning

Dutchman's MINE

The Superstition Mountains of Arizona are sacred to the Native American Apache. The Peralta family operated a gold mine there. The Apache did not like mining in the mountains. In 1848, they killed all but one miner.

The lone survivor escaped to Mexico, taking the secret of the mine's location with him. In the 1860s, a German man named Jacob Waltz arrived in Arizona. He claimed to know the location of the mine. English speakers mistook the German word *Deutsch*, which means German, for the word Dutch, so it was named Dutchman's Mine.

Do the Superstition Mountains hide the secret of the lost mine?

A number of sites claim to be Dutchman's Mine, but no one knows the actual location for certain.

Waltz claimed to have found the mine, but never made his fortune. When he was dying, he told his nurse the mine's location. She searched for years, but never found it.

The Cursed Mountains

In 1954, a tourist found treasure maps carved into rocks in the Superstition Mountains. Gold hunters began to search for the mine again. People are still looking. Some people say an Apache **curse** protects the mountains. Others believe an earthquake in 1987 must have buried the mine— and its gold—forever.

Mystery File: SPANISH TRAIL

The Spanish Trail is an old trade route that ran from New Mexico to California. The trail passes through rugged landscapes rich in precious metals, and is said to be full of lost Spanish mines, dead gold prospectors, and buried treasure.

Mystery words...

curse: a magic spell intended to harm someone

Pirate
TREASURE

Kidd ended up being hanged by the English government for piracy.

Scottish pirate William Kidd captured many ships and tons of treasure. He was a wanted man. Before his arrest, Kidd buried his treasure. The search for the missing chests of gold still goes on.

In 1699, Captain Kidd began to worry that he would be caught and punished by the English. He sailed along the coast of New England, hiding his treasure as he went. Places where he may have buried it include Gardiner's Island, Block Island, Money Cove, and Oak Island. Then he met with the governor of New York. Kidd tried to use the promise of treasure to buy his freedom. His **ploy** failed and he was sentenced to death. He was hanged in London in 1701.

Mystery words...

ploy: a trick to try to accomplish something

Hidden Maps

Over 200 years later, two English brothers bought some furniture that had belonged to Kidd. Hidden inside, they found four treasure maps. Experts confirmed the maps were genuine. Treasure hunters used them to search for Kidd's gold in places as far away as the Caribbean and East Asia. No one found anything. Then in 2007, divers found the wreck of a ship captured by Kidd. They found canons and artifacts—but no gold.

Few treasure maps have ever been found. One of the oldest is said to be the Copper Scroll. It dates from 50 to 100 CE. The French pirate Olivier Levasseur left coded messages in the 1700s about the location of his gold, but no one has cracked the code--yet.

Is Kidd's treasure still hidden beneath a beach somewhere?

EL DORADO

El Dorado is Spanish for "the golden one." The legend tells of a chief in South America covered in gold dust. Over time, people began to think of El Dorado as a place. For decades, Europeans tried in vain to find it.

The Muisca were said to throw gold into Lake Guatavita for the gods.

In 1537, the Spanish **conquistador** Gonzalo Jimenez de Quesada met the Muisca people who lived in the highlands of what is now Colombia, in South America. The Muisca chief was said to be El Dorado. In a ceremony, he covered himself in gold and jumped into a lake, where the gold washed away as an offering to the gods. The Spaniards searched the lake, but found little gold. The story made its wasy to Europe. In 1542, the conquistador Francisco Orellana searched for El Dorado. He didn't find it, but he did discover the Amazon River.

Mystery words...

conquistador: a Spanish soldier who explored the Americas

In 1594 and in 1617, the English sailor Sir Walter Raleigh tried to search for the treasure. But he, too, left Colombia empty-handed.

End of a Legend

In the early 19th century the explorers Alexander Humboldt and Aimé Bonpland traveled to South America. They decided that El Dorado was a myth. The searches ended. In 1969, however, farmers found a sculpture made from gold in a cave near the Colombian city of Bogotá. The sculpture shows a scene similar to the old Muisca ceremony. Perhaps El Dorado was not a myth, after all.

Mystery File: AZTEC GOLD

In the 1500s, Spanish conquistadors conquered the Aztec empire. They seized gold from the emperor, Moctezuma II. But, according to legend, Moctezuma had carried even more gold south. He hid it in the Mayan ruins of Tikal, in the thick jungle.

This gold raft may show the El Dorado ceremony held by the Muisca.

Poverty Island
TREASURE

Legend says that France sent gold by ship from Canada to help the southern states of the Confederacy during the American Civil War (1861-1865). The gold never arrived.

Poverty Island in Lake Michigan may be anything but poor. Some people believe its waters hide $400 million in French gold. They say a ship's crew threw the treasure overboard to stop pirates from stealing it during the Civil War.

Although there are no records of the incident, people have looked for the gold for years. A major treasure hunt happened in the early 1930s.

Diving bells are used by divers who want to explore deep water.

A ship called the *Captain Lawrence* carried a diving bell. The bell-shaped container could hold air underwater, so divers could explore the lake bed. But the ship sank in a storm in 1933. When the wreck was finally found in 1993, no gold was aboard.

Still Searching

Since the 1930s, thousands of divers have searched for the gold. American diver, Richard Bennett, has spent over 45 years searching for the sunken treasure. He believes that the cold waters of Lake Michigan may still contain a remarkable fortune.

Mystery File:
EMPTY WRECK

Not all the shipwrecks in the world hide treasure. In 1996, divers off the coast of North Carolina discovered *Queen Anne's Revenge*, the ship of the pirate Blackbeard. Although they found cannons and **artifacts**, Blackbeard's treasure has never been found.

Mystery words...

artifacts: objects of cultural interest made by craftworkers

Curse of the PHARAOHS

When English archeologist **Howard Carter** uncovered the tomb of the Egyptian pharaoh Tutankhamun, it set off a mysterious chain of events. Several people linked to the find died sudden or mysterious deaths. Was this the curse of Tut?

Carter entered the tomb in November 1922. He found the pharaoh's body lying in a solid gold coffin. The tomb had already been broken into twice, but it was still packed with treasure.

As the last man climbed back out into the sunshine, a sandstorm swirled over the entrance. Was this the spirit of the dead pharaoh leaving?

Tutankhamun's gold coffin was one of the greatest treasures in his tomb.

Mystery words...

archeologist: someone who studies objects from the past

Mysterious Deaths

The legendary curse said to guard all the pharaohs' tombs seemed to strike. English adventurer Lord Carnarvon had funded the expedition. He died suddenly from an infected mosquito bite. His dog also died. Prince Ali Fahmy Bey, a visitor to the tomb, was shot by his wife. Yet Carter, who spent the longest time inside Tut's tomb, lived another 17 years.

Carter and a colleague examine Tutankhamun's mummified body.

Sunken TREASURE

In 2007, an American team of treasure hunters found a shipwreck off the southern coast of Portugal. Its cargo of coins and other gold and silver was worth about $500 million. Experts thought the wreck was that of the Spanish ship, *Nuestra Señora de las Mercedes*. People rushed to claim the treasure.

The British sank the Spanish ship during a battle in 1804.

Underwater exploration teams use high-tech equipment. They use **sonar** to capture undersea images. Unmanned underwater vehicles investigate the seabed and go inside shipwrecks. In future, these tools should make it easier to find sunken treasure.

Treasure is becoming easier to locate on the seabed.

Odyssey, the U.S. team who found the wreck, claimed it lay in international waters. That meant they could claim up to 90 percent of the treasure. But Spain also claimed it. The British had sunk the ship in 1804 as it sailed from Peru, so Peru also claimed the gold.

South American Connection

The case ended up in court. After five years of legal battles, the decision came. In 2012, the court ordered the Americans to return the treasure to Spain. Spanish museums now display the treasure.

Mystery words...

sonar: a system of locating unseen objects using sound waves

A Lucky FIND

When Kevin Elliot and his cousin, Martin, found more than 9,000 ancient Roman coins, called denarii, in a field in England, they struck it rich. Sometimes, all it takes is a little digging.

In 1999, Kevin and Martin Elliot walked across a field with a metal detector. Within a few minutes, they found a coin. In only 90 minutes, the cousins filled several buckets with ancient coins. The coins were silver denarii, dating from around 31 BCE to 224 CE. It was the largest **hoard** of denarii ever found in Britain. It would have been a fortune for a Roman. The sum was probably equal to ten years' pay for a Roman soldier.

Although metal detecting is a popular hobby, few people find buried treasure.

Mystery words...

hoard: a buried or hidden collection of valuable objects

Who Owns the Treasure?

After the Elliots discovered the coins at Shapwick in Somerset, they called in the experts. Archeologists dug at the site. They found the remains of a Roman villa built around a courtyard. The Shapwick treasure and the villa were important archeological discoveries. A court decided that the coins were "treasure trove." That meant that no one had a claim to own them. The Elliots were entitled to keep their discovery. Eventually, the Museum of Somerset paid the cousins over $400,000 for their find.

Mystery File:
BURIED TREASURE

In 1992, Eric Lawes used a metal detector to find Roman treasure at Hoxne in England. Metal detectors also find newer treasures. In 2008, Mike DeMar used an underwater device on a dive off Key West, Florida. He found a golden goblet from a Spanish ship that sank in 1622.

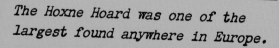

The Hoxne Hoard was one of the largest found anywhere in Europe.

Riddle of the
MONEY PIT

In 1795, three boys found a hole on Oak Island, Nova Scotia, in Canada. As they dug into the pit, they discovered oak planks. The hole had been dug by someone—but why?

A local story said that the pirate Captain Kidd had buried a fortune on Oak Island just before his arrest in 1699. The promise of riches has drawn many treasure hunters to the area. In the 1800s, following the discovery of the pit, excavators began to dig into it. They uncovered deadly traps guarding its secrets. Hidden channels flooded the pit with water.

Captain Kidd's gold still excites treasure hunters after 300 years.

Stone Message

About 90 feet (27 m) into the pit, diggers found a stone slab with mysterious markings. Years later, an expert **deciphered** the message. It read, "Forty feet below, two million pounds are buried." But despite the money spent by fortune hunters, nothing has ever been found. In 2010, the Canadian government tried to ban treasure hunters from the "Money Pit." Today, private investors own the island and continue the search.

Treasure hunting can be dangerous, even deadly. Hidden traps in ancient Egyptian tombs protected their treasures from looters. In China, the tomb of the First Emperor was said to be protected by traps that triggered the firing of poisonous arrows.

Digging continues on Oak Island, although nothing has been found.

Mystery words...

deciphered: figured out the meaning of some words or markings

The Knights'
FORTUNE

In the 12th century, the Knights Templar were a military order of monks. They protected Christian pilgrims in the Holy Land, an area sacred to many religions. The Templars became extremely wealthy and even opened a bank. Then on Friday, October 13, 1307, King Philip IV of France arrested the Templars' leaders.

The Templars were so powerful, even the Pope eventually banned them.

THE HOLY GRAIL

The Knights Templar may have found ancient treasure beneath their headquarters in Jerusalem. If so, the Templars' treasure might include ancient Christian **relics**. It might also include the famous **Holy Grail**, the cup Jesus Christ used at the Last Supper.

The Holy Grail, a cup said to have been used by Jesus Christ, might be among the Templars' treasure.

The Templar bank was said to hold land **deeds**, royal jewels, and gold and silver. The French authorities looked for this hoard. They tortured the Templars to try to find out where it was. The surviving Templars fled, but no one knows where they went. In 1312, the Pope disbanded the Templar order.

Centuries of Searching

The missing treasure has inspired centuries of searching. Some people believe the survivors took it to Portugal. Others believe they buried the treasure at Rosslyn Chapel in Scotland. One clue points to the Money Pit on Oak Island, in Canada. However, no clues have led to the missing fortune.

Mystery words...

deeds: legal documents that prove ownership of something

Bars of SILVER

Pancho Villa was a Mexican bandit and revolutionary. Villa needed money to pay for men and weapons to fight the Spanish. On April 9, 1913, Villa and his men hijacked a train belonging to the Wells Fargo banking and shipping company. They stole 122 bars of silver. The treasure was never seen again.

Pancho Villa helped lead the Mexican Revolution against Spanish rule.

As a young bandit, Pancho Villa hid in the Sierra Madre mountains. Later, he may have returned there to hide his silver. Villa was killed in 1923 and never reclaimed his riches. A cave in the mountains may hold over $24 million of the bandit's treasure.

At least two hoards of Villa's treasure are said to be hidden somewhere in Mexico.

When government forces had reached the train, a shoot-out followed in which both sides lost men. Villa and his men escaped with the silver. One story is that they fled toward Bachiniva, in northern Mexico. When one of Villa's wounded **bandits** died, the gang was said to have buried him by the road, hiding the silver with his body.

Striking a Deal

For decades, the silver seemed to be lost. Then, in the late 1990s, the University of California recovered some old letters. They suggested that Villa sold some silver back to Wells Fargo and used the money to buy arms. The stolen silver was worth over $3 million today. Some of it still might be in the unmarked grave on the road to Bachiniva.

Mystery words...

bandits: criminals who mainly rob from travelers

Confederate
GOLD

A million dollars in gold belonging to the Confederate states in the South went missing at the end of the American Civil War (1861-1865). Only a few coins have ever been found. There are many theories about what happened to the rest.

In 1865, as Confederate forces were facing defeat, they fled their capital at Richmond, Virginia. Before leaving, they emptied the banks of gold and jewels. The fleeing Confederates carried away nearly $1 million worth of treasure. They headed toward Washington, Georgia. To protect the treasure from the North's Union soldiers, guards moved it between trains and wagons. But at some point on the journey, the treasure vanished.

The treasure included U.S. gold dollars made before the war.

Where Is the Gold?

Some stories say the Confederate president Jefferson Davis split the money among his generals. Naval officers could carry the gold safely to England or France. It could have been used to pay for a second Confederate uprising. Other legends say the gold never left Georgia. Union soldiers believed the Confederates buried the gold on the Chennault **Plantation** there. They found nothing. Since then, however, a few gold coins have turned up along roads nearby.

Mystery File: KRUGER'S GOLD

During the Boer War (1899–1902) in South Africa, over $250 million went missing. When the British invaded, the Boer president Paul Kruger fled. It's rumored that Kruger hid the treasure somewhere during his journey into exile in Europe.

Mystery words...

plantation: a large estate for growing crops such as tobacco or cotton

Nazi LOOT

During World War II (1939–1945), the party in power in Germany, called the Nazis, stole art, gold, and jewels from the countries they occupied. Since 1945, treasure hunters have been looking for the loot across Europe. Nazi records suggest they might find crates of gold, famous paintings, and secret bank accounts.

American soldiers discovered a stolen painting hidden inside a mine in Austria.

The Amber Room was decorated with 6 tons (6 tonnes) of amber. This copy of the room was built in 2003.

People told stories about treasure hidden in caves or dumped in lakes. One rumor pointed to Lake Toplitz in Austria. People looked for crates of gold there. Some divers died, and the lake was closed off.

Race for Treasure

Other treasure hunters headed to a forest in the Czech Republic. They had heard stories about the Nazis digging in the forest during the war. Some stories report that more than 500 crates of gold, jewels, and paintings are buried there.

Mystery File:
THE AMBER ROOM

The **Amber** Room was one of Russia's greatest treasures. In World War II, the Nazis stole the entire room. It was first believed to have been destroyed during a bombing raid. Then, in 1997, police found parts of the room in Germany. Is more still hidden somewhere?

Mystery words...

amber: a hard orange stone formed by ancient tree sap

Glossary

amber A hard orange stone formed by ancient tree sap

archeologist Someone who studies objects from the past

artifacts Objects of cultural interest made by craftworkers

bandits Criminals who mainly rob travelers

chests Large, strong wooden boxes used for storage

conquistador A Spanish soldier who explored the Americas

cryptic Unclear or secret meaning

curse A magic spell intended to harm someone

deciphered Figured out the meaning of some words or markings

deeds Legal documents that prove ownership of something

hoard A buried or hidden collection of valuable objects

Holy Grail A legendary cup said to have been used by Jesus Christ at the Last Supper

loot Private property that is stolen from an enemy during a war

occupied Conquered and ruled by enemy forces

pirate A person who attacks and robs ships at sea

plantation A large estate for growing crops such as tobacco or cotton

ploy A trick to try to accomplsh something

relics Objects from the past that are valued for their religious significance

sonar A system of locating unseen objects using sound waves

superstition Belief that has no basis in science

Find Out More

BOOKS

Mason, Paul. *Lost Treasures* (Marvels and Mysteries). Macmillan, 2005.

Peters, Gregory N. *Looking for Lost Treasure* (Real World Adventures). Trailblazers, 2014.

O'Donnell, Liam. *Pirate Treasure: Stolen Riches* (The Real World of Pirates). Capstone Press, 2006.

Pryor, Bonnie. *Captain Hannah Pritchard: The Hunt for Pirate Gold* (Historical Fiction Adventures). Enslow Publishers, 2011.

WEBSITES

America's Lost Treasures
Index of the National Geographic Channel show *America's Lost Treasures*, with clips from the programs.
http://channel.nationalgeographic.com/channel/americas-lost-treasures/episode-guide/

Time for Kids
A report from the kids's edition of *Time* magazine about the recovery of treasure from a sunken ship.
www.timeforkids.com/news/sea-treasure/161986

Sunken Treasures
A list of seven underwater treasures, with photographs and videos.
www.buzzfeed.com/mbvd/7-sunken-treasures-discovered

Index